ANIMALS

Miranda Smith

KINGFISHER

NEW YORK

KINGFISHER
LONDON & NEW YORK

Consultant: David Burnie

Illustrations by Polygone Studio/contactjupiter.com
Yvan Meunier/contactjupiter.com
Peter Bull Art Studio

First published in 2009 by Kingfisher
First published in paperback in 2012 by Kingfisher

Distributed in the U.S. and Canada by Macmillan,
175 Fifth Ave., New York, NY 10010

LIBRARY OF CONGRESS CATALOGING-IN-PUBLICATION DATA
Kent, Peter, 1957–
Navigators animals / by Peter Kent.
p. cm.
Includes bibliographical references and index.
1. Technology—Juvenile literature. 2. Science—Juvenile literature. I. Title.
T48.K47 2009
600—dc22

ISBN: 978-0-7534-6746-6

Kingfisher books are available for special promotions and premiums. For details contact:
Special Markets Department, Macmillan, 175 Fifth Avenue, New York, NY 10010.

For more information, please visit www.kingfisherbooks.com

Printed in China
3 5 7 9 8 6 4 2 1

1TR/0911/UTD/WKT/140MA

Note to readers: The website addresses listed in this book are correct at the time of publishing.
However, due to the ever-changing nature of the Internet, website addresses and content can change.
Websites can contain links that are unsuitable for children. The publisher cannot be held responsible for
changes in website addresses or content or for information obtained through third-party websites.
We strongly advise that Internet searches are supervised by an adult.

The Publisher would like to thank the following for permission to reproduce their images (t = top, b = bottom, c = center, r = right, l = left):

Front cover (panda) Frank Lane Picture Agency (FLPA)/Minden; (elephant) Alamy/Steve Bloom; back cover Getty/Digital Vision; page 1 Polygone Studios; 2–3 Polygone Studios; 4tl Still Pictures/ Manfred Danegger; 4tr Photolibrary/Hermann D; 4br Naturepl/Brandon Cole; 5 Naturepl/Tony Heald; 5tr Seapics/Richard Herrmann; 5br Photoshot/NHPA; 6–7 Polygone Studios; 6tr Photolibrary/ David Welling; 6bl Alamy/Steve Bloom; 7t all Naturepl/Mark Payne-Gill; 8–9 Yvan Meunier; 8bl FLPA/Frank Stober; 9tl FLPA/Minden/Michael Durham; 9tr Photolibrary; 10–11 Naturepl/T. J. Rich; 10lc Getty/NGS; 11tr Seapics/Michael S. Nolan; 11b Peter Bull; 12–13 Polygone Studios; 13bl Photoshot/NHPA; 13tc Photolibrary/Thorsten Milse; 14–15 Polygone Studios; 14c Steve Bloom; 15tl Newspix; 15cr FLPA/Minden/Mitsuaki Iwago; 15br Photoshot/Westend61; 16tr Peter Bull; 16bl Naturepl/Rolf Nussbaumer; 16–17 Photolibrary/Ifa; 17tl FLPA/Minden/Tim Fitzharris; 17tr, 17cr and 17br Naturepl/Charlie Hamilton James; 17bl Photolibrary/Michael Dick; 17bc Naturepl/Bernard Castelein; 17br Photolibrary/Herbert Kehrer; 18tl Alamy/William Leaman; 18br Photoshot/Woodfall Wild Images; 18–19 Photolibrary/Roy Toft; 19tl and 19tr Naturepl/David Pike; 19br NGS/Tim Laman; 20l Nicky Studdart; 20tr Naturepl/Richard du Toit; 20br Ardea/Dominic Usher; 21tr Nicky Studdart; 21bl Photolibrary/Fritz Poelking; 21br Photoshot/NHPA; 22–23 Polygone Studios; 22l Photolibrary/Thorsten Milse; 22tr Photolibrary/Ifa; 23t FLPA/Andrew Forsyth; 24–25 Yvan Meunier; 25tr FLPA/Christian Kapteyn; 25bl Photoshot/NHPA/Anthony Bannister; 26tl Naturepl/Tim Macmillan/John Downer Productions; 26b Photolibrary/Dani/Jeske; 26tr Getty Images; 26rb Naturepl/Barry Mansell; 27tl Photoshot/NHPA; 27tr FLPA/Jurgen & Christine Sohns; 27c Photolibrary/Frank & Joyce Burek; 27bl Photoshot/NHPA; 28–29 Polygone Studios; 29cr Alamy/Scott Camazine; 29b Natural Sciences Image Lib (NSIL) New Zealand; 30t Corbis/Lynda Richardson; 30cl Seapics; 30tr Seapics/Masa Ushioda; 30c Photolibrary; 30b Naturepl/Michael Pitts; 31t FLPA/Minden/Michael & Patricia Fogden; 31c Naturepl/Anup Shah; 31b Naturepl/Anup Shah; 32t FLPA/Roger Wilmshurst; 32tl FLPA/Minden/Rene Krekelsura; 32tr Naturepl/Premaphotos; 32c Naturepl/Wilhelm Kolvoort; 32br FLPA/Minden/Rene Krekelsura; 33c FLPA/Derek Middleton; 33br Alamy/Blickwinkel; 34–35t Corbis/Joe McDonald; 34b Photolibrary/Berndt; 35tr Naturepl/Jane Burton; 35b Photolibrary/Brian Kenney; 36–37 Seapics/Masa Ushioda; 36c Seapics/Masa Ushioda; 36b Seapics/David B. Fleetham; 37c Peter Bull; 37tc Naturepl/Georgette Douwma; 37r Shutterstock; 37r FLPA/R Dirscherl; 37b Seapics/Edward G. Lines; 38–39 Yvan Meunier; 39tl Science Photo Library/Peter Scoones; 39b Imagequest Marine; 40–41 Naturepl/Doug Perrine; 40tl Naturepl/Jose B. Ruiz; 41cr Science Photo Library/Laguna Design; 41b Corbis/Dan Guravich; 42cl FLPA/Minden/Michael & Patricia Fogden; 42b Photoshot/NHPA; 42r Shutterstock; 43t Naturepl/Hans Christoph Kappel; 43c Shutterstock; 43b NGS/Paul Zahl; 48tl Shutterstock/ANP; 48tr Alamy/Paul Weaver; 48cl Art Archive/Victoria & Albert Museum; 48cr Murray Robbins; 48bl Corbis/Paul Souders; 48l Shutterstock/photo-art

CONTENTS

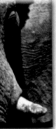

EVOLVED—*gradually changed over time to fit a particular way of life*

Reptiles

Reptiles are cold-blooded vertebrates with tough, scaly skin. They breathe air and live on land and in water. Most reptiles lay eggs, but some give birth to live young. Their body shapes vary greatly—from long, legless cobras (above) to shell-covered turtles.

Birds

These vertebrates walk on two feet, are warm-blooded, and lay eggs. They rule the skies, having evolved feathers, wings, and a lightweight skeleton for flight. Birds have beaks and range from meat-eating birds of prey, such as this barn owl, to hummingbirds that sip nectar from flowers.

Fish

Covered with scales, these vertebrates are able to move easily through the water they live in, maneuvering their streamlined bodies with their fins. They take oxygen from the water using gills. Most fish lay eggs, but some, such as the great white shark (right), give birth to live young.

WORLD OF ANIMALS

Animals inhabit every nook and cranny on Earth. Some are vertebrates (animals with backbones), but the vast majority are invertebrates (animals with no backbone). Most animals, including invertebrates and reptiles, are cold-blooded, which means that their body temperature is determined by their surroundings. Warm-blooded birds and mammals are able to make and maintain their own body heat. All animals get the energy they need from the food they eat.

Nearly two million species of animals have been identified, and 97 percent of them are invertebrates.

Invertebrates

These animals do not have a backbone or an internal skeleton made of bone. They are an incredibly large and varied group. Some, such as jellyfish (below), have soft bodies. Others, such as insects and mollusks, have hard outer cases or shells.

Mammals

Although most mammals live on land, some fly and swim. All of these vertebrates, except for monotremes, give birth to live young that feed on milk produced by the female. Mammals range in size from the tiny bumblebee bat to the enormous African elephant (left).

Amphibians

Most of these cold-blooded vertebrates start life in the water, as larvae that breathe using gills. As they grow, the larvae change shape, becoming adults that breathe using lungs, like this tree frog (right).

ATTACK AND DEFENSE

Mammals are successful because they are very adaptable. Some predators, such as lions, work together to take down prey, while others, including tigers, are lone hunters. Camouflage (blending into the background) is a great defense against predators. Herds provide protection for weaker members—for example, musk oxen form defensive rings around their young when threatened.

"The scientific name of an animal that doesn't either run from or fight its enemies is lunch."

Michael Friedman (born 1960)
American poet

Best defense

When a wolf snarls, it is a terrifying sight—enough to make most attackers take to their heels. By displaying their teeth in this way, wolves have found a very effective method of defense.

Distracting patterns

The black-and-white markings on a zebra are unique to that individual animal. When a herd of zebras is moving together, it is hard for a predator, such as a crocodile, to make out where one animal ends and another begins. This patterning is called disruptive coloration, and it is a superb defense.

> Green algae growing in the fur of sloths helps camouflage them in the rainforest.

⊖ ARMORED BALL

When threatened, an armadillo—Spanish for "little armored one"—rolls up into a ball. Its soft underside is protected by the bony, skin-covered armor on the top of its body and tail. Pangolins protect themselves in a similar fashion: their upper bodies are covered with overlapping scales. The hedgehog, by contrast, has spines all over its back and sides and forms a prickly ball.

three-banded armadillo

hinged back allows flexibility

defensive ball is impenetrable

www.uen.org/utahlink/activities/view_activity.cgi?activity_id-3803

Hunting as a team

The chimpanzees that live in the forests of West Africa eat fruit, leaves, and nuts, but they also hunt monkeys. The monkeys are smaller and able to leap onto branches that would break under the chimpanzees' weight. The male hunters have found that they can catch their prey by working as a team.

KEY

1 Red colobus monkeys

2 Driver chimpanzee at rear makes sure monkeys keep moving

3 Clearly visible blocker prevents monkeys from changing direction

4 Second blocker hoots and screams, cutting off escape

5 Chaser joins in the hunt

6 Second chaser rushes up a tree to join in

7 Ambusher anticipates where the monkeys will move, only showing himself at the last minute

ECHOLOCATION—*a method of locating prey by emitting sounds that echo back*

FINDING FOOD

To keep warm, to grow, and to give their bodies energy, mammals need to eat. The smaller the mammals, the quicker they lose body heat, so it is important to eat frequently—in the case of shrews, almost all day long. Carnivores scavenge upon or hunt other animals; herbivores eat plants; and omnivores eat both plants and animals. And sometimes, because of the weather or time of year, food can be hard to find.

> "All animals are equal, but some animals are more equal than others."
>
> **George Orwell (1903–1950)**
> *British author, from his novel* Animal Farm *(1945)*

A nose for ants

The giant anteater of South and Central America has an acute sense of smell, which leads it to a termite mound or anthill. It breaks into the sandy walls of the mound with sharp claws, making a hole that is large enough for its long, narrow snout and tongue. The anteater may lap up as many as 35,000 termites and ants a day from several mounds.

Hunting on the wing

A bat finds its prey by using echolocation to determine its shape, size, distance, and direction of travel. The mammal emits high-pitched sounds that bounce as echoes off objects. The bat listens to the echoes and homes in on moths and other prey.

claws are tucked under to
protect them while walking

Treetop feeders

The tallest of all the animals that live on land, the giraffe has evolved to feed at a level that is out of reach for other herbivores. Its favorite food on the grasslands of Africa is the thorny acacia tree. The giraffe's long neck, which is made up of seven elongated vertebrae, allows it to browse the topmost branches.

> The smallest mammal in the world is the Savi's pygmy shrew, which is 2 in. (6cm) long from nose to tip of tail.

◉ TINY ANIMAL, BIG APPETITE

Shrews are aggressive hunters that forage for anything, from seeds and spiders to small mammals and birds. They have a high metabolism and need to eat 80–90 percent of their own body weight each day. Most have poor eyesight and locate prey by smell. Like bats, whales, dolphins, and some birds, certain shrew species give ultrasonic squeaks, using echolocation to target prey.

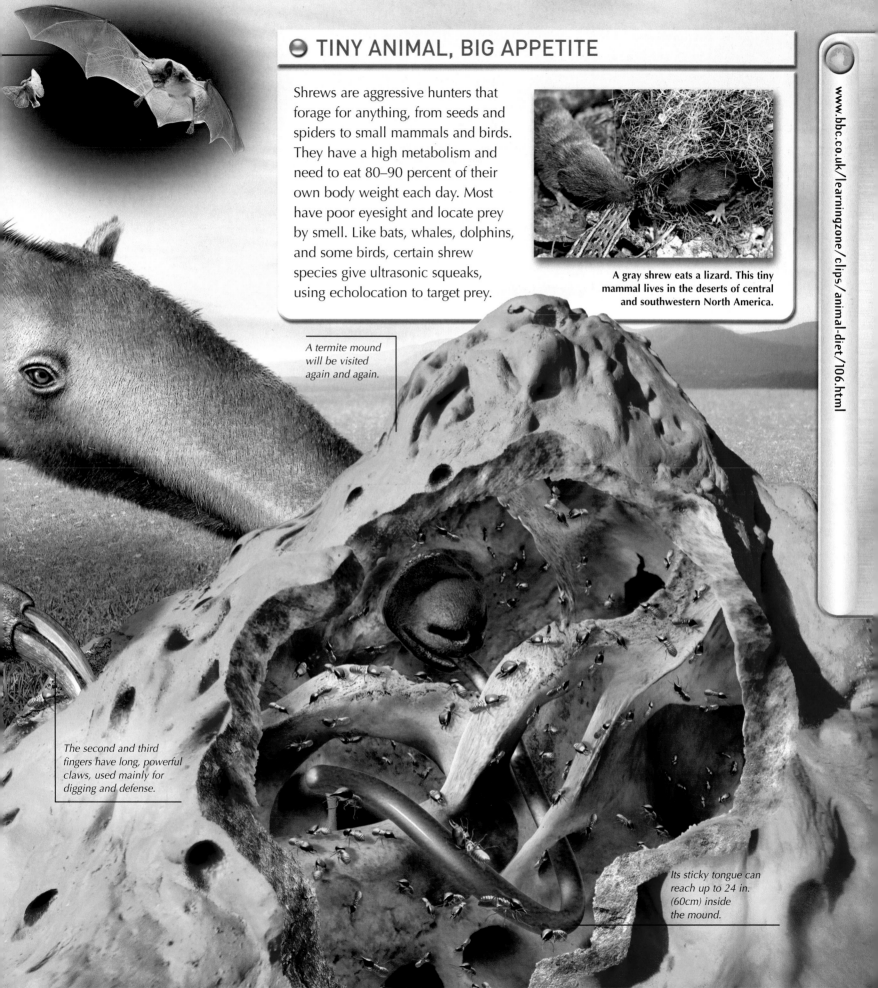

A gray shrew eats a lizard. This tiny mammal lives in the deserts of central and southwestern North America.

www.bbc.co.uk/learningzone/clips/animal-diet/106.html

A termite mound will be visited again and again.

The second and third fingers have long, powerful claws, used mainly for digging and defense.

Its sticky tongue can reach up to 24 in. (60cm) inside the mound.

STORAGE AND DIGESTION

Many animals need to store food, either in a safe place or inside their own bodies, because of the extreme conditions of their habitats. In all cases, the food needs to be broken down before the nutrients can be absorbed. The majority of animals bite and chew food before digesting it, while others, such as flatworms, absorb nutrients through their bodies.

RUMINANT—*hoofed mammal with a specialized digestive system and two stomachs*

Hoarding food

The African leopard is a very strong animal. It has a large head on muscular shoulders and can weigh up to 200 lbs. (90kg). This strong, agile meat eater is capable of climbing a 50-ft. (15-m)-high tree with a large, dead springbok as heavy as itself in its mouth. It drags its prey there to keep it safe from scavenging lions and hyenas.

The camel's hump
Camels are well adapted to living in areas of the world where food is sometimes scarce. Their humps store fat, a fuel for their bodies to use when needed.

A camel can go with little to no food or water for up to seven days.

Bubble nets can be up to 100 ft. (30m) in diameter.

Humpback whales form nets of bubbles around shoals of fish and krill. The whales then surface through the shoal with their mouths open, swallowing their prey.

Hairy whalebone plates filter the fish and krill out of the seawater.

Whale restaurant

In their search for food, many humpback whales visit the cold Pacific waters off the coast of Alaska. They spend several months at this rich feeding ground, eating as much as they can. They have to put on enough weight to be able to live off their fat reserves for the rest of the year.

The leopard hunts at night and often suffocates its prey by clamping its jaws over the animal's nose.

⊖ INSIDE A RUMINANT'S STOMACH

Although plants, especially grasses, are often easy to find, they are very hard to digest. Many herbivores have bacteria inside their bodies that help release nutrients from tough plant matter. Ruminants such as buffalo have four chambers in their first stomach. The largest, the rumen, contains millions of these bacteria.

rumen
reticulum
omasum
abomasum

The dark bands around the eyes reduce glare from the sun.

LIVING UNDERGROUND

Burrows offer shelter to animals, protecting them from predators and extreme heat or cold. Many mammals—including moles, gophers, groundhogs, rabbits, badgers, and foxes—dig out burrows or dens underground. Some, such as the naked mole rat, live permanently in their burrows, while others use them mainly at night or to give birth or escape danger.

On the alert

Meerkats live on the southern African plains in large groups. They dig out six to 15 burrows in the sands of the Kalahari desert and move from one to another to forage for insects and other food. The burrows have several tunnels at different depths, leading to cool sleeping chambers.

> HIBERNATION—*when an animal spends the winter in a dormant state*

Frozen den

In late autumn, a pregnant female polar bear digs a den in a snowdrift along a mountain slope or on sea ice. In November or December, she gives birth, usually to two cubs. Body heat and the insulation of the snow keep the bears warm until they emerge from hibernation in March or April.

KEY

1. Lookout on mound warns of danger from hunting birds and other predators
2. Up to 70 entrance holes per burrow
3. Using front claws as a shovel to dig out new passageways
4. Markings on back are unique to each meerkat
5. Pups stay in burrow for about three weeks before venturing out
6. Sleeping cuddled together for warmth

Rodent tunnel dwellers

Naked mole rats spend their whole life seeking out tubers underground in the sandy soils of East Africa. They can hardly see, and when they meet another mole rat in a tunnel, they squeeze over or under and continue on their way. They can travel backward as easily as they can move forward.

Females give birth to up to four pups each year in a breeding burrow.

When digging, meerkats are able to close their ears to keep out the dirt.

Flying high

The nocturnal flying lemur, or colugo, has a face that looks like that of a lemur, but it is unique: it is not related to any living species. It is well adapted to life high up in the rainforests of Southeast Asia and the Philippines. If threatened, it simply spreads its limbs, stretching out a membrane of skin that allows it to glide down to safety.

A flying lemur weighs only about 1.2 oz. (35g) at birth.

Philippine flying lemur can glide up to 330 ft. (100m)

Water birth

A female hippopotamus usually gives birth underwater, pushing the newly born calf to the surface so it can breathe. She stays in the water without eating for several days, only leaving to graze when the baby is strong enough. Baby hippos drink their mother's milk for up to eight months.

membrane reaches from neck to tip of tail

GIVING BIRTH

Monotremes are mammals that lay eggs, and only two animals belong to this group, the duck-billed platypus and the echidna. All other mammals are viviparous—they give birth to live young. The young of placental mammals, including humans, develop inside their mother's womb before being born. Marsupials, including kangaroos, give birth to young at a very early stage, and the babies need special protection to survive outside the womb.

> Baby dolphins are born tail first, unlike other mammals, which are usually born headfirst.

Echidnas live in Australia.

The egg hatches after 10 days.

Mammal eggs

The short-nosed echidna (spiny anteater) is a monotreme. The female develops a backward-facing pouch on her underside and lays a single leathery egg in it. The baby echidna, or puggle, feeds from a special patch on her skin that secretes milk.

baby clings to mother's belly as she glides

baby takes 2–3 years to reach adult size

⊖ A LONG FIRST JOURNEY

When a baby kangaroo, or joey, is born, it is only 0.8 in. (2cm) long. The marsupial has to haul itself all the way up its mother's body and into a pouch, where there are four teats. It attaches itself to one of them and stays there for several weeks, feeding on its mother's rich milk. There may be multiple joeys of different ages in the pouch at the same time.

The joey will leave the pouch completely by the time it is 10 months old.

Tiger, tiger

Tigers give birth to a litter of up to four cubs. They are born blind and helpless, and they stay on their own for long periods while their mother is hunting for food. The cubs stay with their mother for up to two years, learning hunting skills from her.

HUNTING SKILLS

There are no more expert hunters than the birds of prey. They hunt from the air, using their keen senses of sight and hearing to target prey—eagles, for example, can spot a moving rabbit at a distance of 2 mi. (3km). Peregrines stoop at an incredible 200 mph (320km/h), striking with sharp talons and killing by impact. The nocturnal barn owl is able to find its mouse prey in complete darkness.

Flight feathers are long and stiff, giving the bird lift and allowing it to maneuver.

barbule

barb

Closely linked barbs and barbules form a smooth surface for flight.

Snatching prey

The poise and control of the hunting bird can be seen clearly when the magnificent osprey catches its favorite fish food. It flies low over the water's surface, then plunges feet first, sometimes right into the water, its talons outstretched to snatch up a fish.

Absolute control

The smaller a hummingbird is, the faster its wings beat. When a 4-in. (10-cm)-long buff-bellied hummingbird sips nectar from a flower, its wings beat an amazing 40 times per second. These birds' wings allow them to fly forward, up and down, sideways, and backward.

reversible outer toe holds muscular prey while pointing forward

Hummingbirds have such control that they can hover on the spot.

> The Australian pelican has the longest beak, at up to 18.5 in. (47cm).

Powerful scavenger

Like vultures, marabou storks have naked heads and necks, adaptations for scavenging. These large birds are up to 55 in. (140cm) high and weigh up to 18 lbs. (8kg). They seek out all kinds of prey, both alive and dead, and if their heads were covered in feathers, it would be difficult to keep them clean.

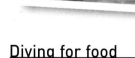

The Eurasian kingfisher has dazzling blue-and-orange plumage.

primary feathers propel the bird through the air

wingspan of up to 5.6 ft. (1.7m)

secondary flight feathers give the bird lift

strongly curved beak used to tear fish apart

BEAK SHAPES

All birds have beaks that are specially adapted to find the food that will enable them to survive in a particular environment. For example, some have hard tips to kill prey or crack nuts, while others have sensitive tips to locate food by touch.

A parrot's strong, curved beak breaks in to nuts and fruit to extract the seeds.

A pelican dives, using its pouch as a fishing net. It tips its beak to drain the water and then eats the fish whole.

The flamingo swings its upside-down beak from side to side in water, filtering out small food items.

Diving for food

Kingfishers have a dramatic hunting method. They sit still on a branch above a stream, waiting for signs of movement. Then they dive swiftly and steeply into the water, capturing the fish in their dagger-shaped beak at a depth of no more than 10 in. (25cm). They beat their wings to resurface, returning to their perch to eat their prey.

Each individual adult male lazuli bunting has his own song.

The power of song

In the spring, stimulated by the days getting longer, many birds sing vigorously and nonstop. It is the beginning of the mating season, and they sing to defend their territory and attract a mate. Each species has its own song, and how the male sings will decide whether or not he is successful.

wingspan of up to 8 ft. (2.5m)

ATTRACTING A MATE

Male birds use various techniques to attract a mate. Peacocks show off spectacular plumage, and red kites dive and swoop acrobatically in flight. Grebes "rush" across water together, while woodpeckers drum rhythmically on hollow tree trunks. Bowerbirds build structures, and Adélie penguins give pebbles as gifts. Many birds use songs to find a mate—the tiny wren achieves an amazing 740 notes a minute and can be heard at a distance of 1,640 ft. (500m)!

⊖ CHANGING SHAPE

Size is an important factor in the mating game. The male great frigate bird inflates a magnificent red chest pouch, and the tragopan of western China inflates its blue wattle. The male turkey's whole head changes color when it becomes excited, and its wattle also swells.

A male wild turkey swells its wattle in display.

 The Australian superb lyrebird mimics the mating calls of at least 20 other bird species.

Heads thrust back, two red-crowned cranes perform on the lek, or mating ground.

The cranes call, mirroring each other's movements.

The courtship dance includes a series of bows, head bobs, and leaps.

males and females look alike

Colorful display

There are 42 species of birds of paradise, and the males have some of the most colorful plumage in the world. In Papua New Guinea, natives have used the tail feathers of males as ceremonial decorations for centuries.

Dazzling dancers

Cranes have been adopted by many cultures as symbols of fidelity and love. Once they have bonded, they stay together for life. Their body language is very elaborate, and they have at least 90 different displays. They dance at all ages, and there are particular dances for courtship and breeding.

"A bird does not sing because it has an answer. It sings because it has a song."

Chinese proverb

HOME BUILDERS

INCUBATION—the warming of eggs to hatch them

Birds need somewhere to incubate and hatch their eggs. Some build structures, such as the blackbird's cup-shaped grass nest. Ducks lay their eggs in shallow depressions in sand, vegetation, or soil. Woodpeckers drill holes in trees, and shearwaters dig burrows by the ocean. The mallee fowl builds a large mound of leaves, adjusting the temperature by adding or scraping away materials as necessary.

The male Cape weaver first winds grasses and reeds around a branch.

He threads the branch with grasses to form a circular structure between 3.3 ft. (1m) and 33 ft. (10m) above the ground.

Rooftop nest

White storks are famous for the large, untidy nests that they build on top of roofs, towers, tall trees, cliff edges, and telephone poles. The birds pair for life and return to the same nest year after year, adding to the nest each time. Some older nests are very large.

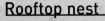

 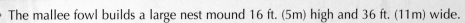

Weaving a home

Weaverbirds build the most elaborate nests of any bird. Different species use different materials and create a variety of shapes. For example, sociable weavers build giant, multichambered nests, with room for up to 100 families. The Cape weaver of South Africa uses its long, pointed beak to weave a round nest with a downward-facing entrance.

www.biokids.umich.edu/guides/tracks_and_sign/build/birdnests/

Burrowing birds

The only time Atlantic puffins spend on land is to nest. They dig out burrows in the soil of grassy cliffs, lining the nest with grass, feathers, or seaweed. They produce a single egg, and both parents look after the chick until it fledges.

The entrance to the weaverbird's finished nest faces downward. Inside, the female lays two to five eggs that she incubates for about two weeks.

Both male and female parents feed the chicks.

Mud structures

Barn swallows build cup-shaped nests from mud pellets found in puddles or wet soil. They carry the pellets in their beaks, making up to 1,000 trips. The nests are often built in barns or under the eaves of a house and are lined with grasses and feathers or other soft materials.

FLEDGLING—*a young bird that has grown flight feathers and is ready to fly*

RAISING YOUNG

Birds have evolved strategies to give their young the best chance of survival. There is safety in numbers—crowding together in large colonies works well. Many birds lay large clutches of eggs or have several batches of young each year. This ensures that even if some chicks die, others will survive to adulthood. Within hours of hatching, many fledglings instinctively follow their parents on food-finding expeditions.

⊖ CUCKOO IN THE NEST

Some cuckoos make another species hatch and take care of their chicks. For example, a cuckoo may lay an egg in a warbler's nest. The egg resembles the host's eggs, but the cuckoo chick hatches earlier and grows faster. Often the cuckoo chick pushes the eggs or other hatchlings out of the nest while the parent warblers feed it as if it were their own.

A cuckoo fledgling is fed by its warbler "parent."

"In all things of nature there is something of the marvelous."

Aristotle (384–322 B.C.)
Greek philosopher, from his work On the Parts of Animals *(350 B.C.)*

Babies on ice

Chicks in the open are in danger of attack from predators. Emperor penguin chicks are also threatened by the icy cold of Antarctica. The parents take turns to keep first the egg and then the newly hatched chick safe and warm tucked in above their feet.

unhatched coot chick in egg

distinctive fluffy orange-and-blue head

Father's footsteps

By the time a baby ostrich is a day old, it can eat and walk, and its one aim is to follow the long legs of its parent. If one male with its offspring meets another, they tend to fight. The loser runs away so fast that its young cannot keep up. Instead, they follow the victor, who suddenly finds himself with an expanded family!

The aggressive Eurasian coot lives on lakes and rivers throughout Europe, Africa, Asia, and Australia.

Nesting on water

Coots build tall nests of dried grasses in reed beds or on underwater obstacles in the middle of lakes and rivers. They lay up to 15 speckled eggs in a clutch, but only a few chicks survive. The rest are taken by predators (such as foxes), starve to death, or are killed by their own parents when food is scarce.

The parent feeds very young chicks insect larvae, seeds, and plants.

egg tooth is used to chip hole in eggshell

www.pbs.org/lifeofbirds/home/index.html

The 24-in. (60-cm)-long Gila monster lives in North America and has a large tail to store fat, on which it can live for months at a time.

legs are set in the sides of the body

alternate legs move together

lizard "tastes" air with its tongue

short, sturdy legs and long claws for digging

UNDER THE SKIN

Locomotion in reptiles depends on what is happening under the skin. Snakes have no legs, so they use their ribs and muscles to slither along the ground or move from branch to branch. Some snakes "sidewind" on sand, throwing themselves across the loose surface diagonally. Reptiles such as lizards are more slow and restricted, using their strong limbs and tails to move. On land, the slowest of all are the armored turtles and tortoises.

Walk like a lizard

Lizards, including this Gila monster, move more like a fish than a mammal. They sway as they walk, and the muscles that move their bodies from side to side are the same ones that help them breathe. They are not able to run as efficiently as mammals. Lizards are good at running in short bursts, but only if their bodies are warm. If they are cold, they move much more slowly.

 ❯ Some basilisk lizards can run away on their hind legs across the water's surface when threatened.

⊖ VERTICAL RUN

Geckos are impressive climbers. They are able to run vertically up most surfaces and even upside down across overhanging areas. They have flattened pads at the ends of their toes that are covered with millions of microscopic hairs called setae, each split into branches. These help "glue" the lizards to almost any surface.

Tokay geckos are often seen running up and down the walls of houses in Southeast Asia, chasing the insects and small invertebrates that they eat.

unlike with most lizards, tail does not grow back when broken

Gila monsters live in scrubland and desert, burrowing into thickets and under rocks to find moisture and escape the heat.

long, flexible spine

Changing skin

Both snakes and lizards molt or "slough" regularly to replace old or damaged outer skin. Most lizards lose their skin in flakes over a period of days. Snakes, such as this common tiger snake, crawl out of their old skin all at once, turning it inside out and leaving it in one piece.

Gila monster can give a venomous bite

Venom is produced in salivary glands in the lizard's lower jaw, and its poisonous bite is used to defend itself.

Glides over distances of up to 200 ft. (60m) have been recorded.

Flying from danger

When this tree-dwelling flying lizard is threatened, it has an unusual method of escape. It has elongated ribs with skin stretched between them, which act like wings as it glides from tree to tree. When the lizard is at rest, the ribs fold against the body.

AVOIDING PREDATORS

Reptiles have varied ways of protecting themselves. Like other animals, they often run away, climb trees, or fight back when attacked. However, many are superbly camouflaged and are even able to change color. Some lizards can shed part of their tail if seized, growing a new one in its place. Reptiles such as the frilled lizard can make themselves look bigger, and the hard shells of turtles and tortoises are an effective defense.

⊖ WARNING COLORATION

When strong contrasting colors are seen on an animal, they usually warn that the animal is dangerous. Most of the nonvenomous milk snakes have bright red, black, and yellow bands. These colors mimic those of the highly venomous coral snake, and the milk snake sometimes even copies the coral snake's behavior to scare away predators.

Milk snakes can be up to 55 in. (140cm) long.

The western coral snake grows up to 21 in. (53cm) long.

"A chameleon doesn't leave one tree until he's sure of another."

Arabian proverb

A thorny problem

The thorny devil's color changes from pale browns when warm to darker colors when cold, and this camouflage is very effective in the deserts of Australia. However, it is slow-moving and would be vulnerable to predators if it were not covered all over with sharp spines.

The thorny devil rocks back and forth as it walks.

> Texas horned lizards squirt blood from ducts near their eyes at predators up to 10 ft. (3m) away.

The distinctive curled muscular tail has adapted to grasp and balance.

Masters of disguise

Panther chameleons can be found all over the island of Madagascar, off the southeast coast of Africa. They vary in color, and the males are generally more brightly colored than the females. Like all chameleons, they change color in response to changes in temperature, light, or mood.

A brightly colored adult male panther chameleon.

http://kids.nationalgeographic.com/kids/photos/gallery/animal-camouflage/

Chameleons are difficult to spot in leafy rainforest habitat.

Faking death

One defensive mechanism used by some animals when threatened is to play dead. A reptile that does this very effectively is the shy and elusive grass snake. It becomes completely limp, turning on its back with its mouth open and tongue lolling out.

REPTILE SENSES

"Use your enemy's hand
to catch a snake."

Persian proverb

Most reptiles are skilled at spotting moving prey, but there are some, such as blind snakes, that have poor eyesight because they live underground. Snakes do not have an ear opening and can hear only very low sounds, feeling the sound through their bodies as they slither along. Many reptiles use their tongue to touch, and some snakes use it to taste.

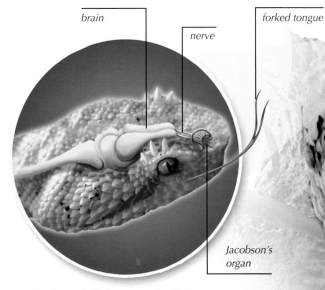

brain

nerve

forked tongue

Jacobson's organ

The viper's forked tongue rubs off the scents it has collected onto the Jacobson's organ in the roof of the mouth. The organ analyzes the scents and sends a message to the brain.

A slender anole is quite unaware of the danger it is in. One lunge by the viper, and it is all over.

The deeper the fork in the tongue, the more the Jacobson's organ is used.

> Special ligaments in a snake's jaw allow it to swallow prey many times larger than the size of its head.

The eyelash viper uses its strong, prehensile tail to grip onto the branch as it launches its body through the air toward its prey.

Sensing food

An eyelash viper—so called because of the spiny scales over each eye—strikes, its mouth open to give a venomous bite. The forked tongue, flicking in and out and tasting the air, has detected the scent of potential prey. On the front of its face, heat sensors called pits have indicated the exact location and size of the anole lizard.

Hunting with a lure

There are two red structures on the tip of an alligator snapping turtle's tongue. They wriggle like small worms, acting as a lure for swimming prey. All this North American turtle has to do is sit on the bottom of a river with its mouth open and wait for a fish to swim in.

⊖ A THIRD EYE

New Zealand's tuataras are called "living fossils" because they have hardly changed in 200 million years. They have a tiny third "eye" on top of their head. It is visible in hatchlings but is soon covered with scales. The eye is connected to the pineal gland and may, by interpreting the amount of light falling on it, trigger sleep and hibernation.

EMBRYO—the early stage of an animal's development before it is hatched or born

The tiny, newly hatched loggerhead turtles rush toward the water.

PARENTAL SKILLS

Reptiles produce young in a variety of ways. Most lay eggs, but some lizards and snakes give birth to live young. The sex of the reptile is often determined by how warm the eggs are during their incubation hidden in soil or vegetation. Some lizards take care of their young after birth, and crocodiles are famous for their gentle care of whole nurseries of young crocodiles.

Digging to the surface

Every two or three years, loggerhead turtles lay their eggs in holes that they dig in the sand. They lay about 100 eggs in three to five nests. The mothers then return to the ocean. After an incubation of about 60 days, the young hatch and dig themselves out.

Hatching out

The nocturnal, desert-dwelling leopard gecko lays clutches of one or two tough, leathery-shelled eggs. The eggs are incubated in sand or in a rock crevice to shelter them from the heat of the day and the cold of the night. They hatch six to 12 weeks later.

Two female whiptail lizards on a cactus.

All female

Whiptail lizards live in the deserts and scrublands of North America. Some whiptail species consist only of females. They act out malelike mating behavior and then lay eggs that produce young. The young are clones—they are genetically identical to the mother. This process is called parthenogenesis.

> Snakes are not good parents—only a few species of pythons actually incubate their eggs.

⊜ GIVING BIRTH TO LIVE YOUNG

Most snakes are oviparous, which means they lay eggs. Some species, however, give birth to live young. They keep the eggs inside their bodies, and, in some cases, the embryos feed through a kind of placenta. Viviparous snakes include vipers, boas, pipe snakes, and sea snakes.

female hog-nosed viper giving birth

young snake being born

A mother Nile crocodile tenderly carries a hatchling to the water.

Gentle parent

Nile crocodiles dig holes to incubate their eggs. Unlike turtles, they guard their nests and attack anything that threatens them. When the babies are ready to hatch, they chirp, and the mother tears open the nest. Both parents may gently roll the eggs in their mouths and squeeze them until the young hatch.

Nile crocodiles lay up to 80 eggs at one time.

1. Egg and embryo

After fertilization by the male great crested newt and a short incubation period, the eggs are deposited by the female over several weeks. The eggs are attached either singly or in clumps to underwater plants, sometimes with a leaf folded over them for protection.

Just before it hatches, the embryo can be seen clearly through the egg casing.

Eggs in foam

In Africa, female great gray tree frogs create extraordinary nests on branches over water. The female churns fluid that she produces into a large white foam ball, into which she deposits her eggs. The male then fertilizes the eggs, and they develop inside the foam nest for about five days. When the tadpoles hatch, they fall into the water below.

The larvae live in water, eating algae, small invertebrates, or other tadpoles.

2. Egg to larva

The eggs hatch after about three weeks. The great crested newt larvae, or tadpoles, are distinctive because they have black blotches over the body, tail, and crest. This is a risky time for the young newts, as they often become a tasty meal for fish.

The eft has bushy gills and is yellow in color.

LIFE CYCLES

Amphibians—frogs, toads, salamanders, newts, and the wormlike caecilians—are cold-blooded vertebrates. Most of them spend part of their life in water breathing with gills, and part on land breathing with lungs. There are three stages in an amphibian's life cycle: egg, larva, and adult. Most species lay their eggs in water. Some eggs, however, develop inside the animal's body, and some species lay eggs on land.

 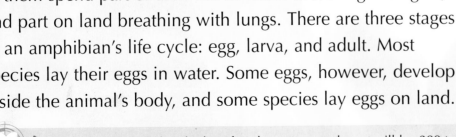

> Between March and mid-July, a female great crested newt will lay 200 to 300 eggs.

Growing stages

The life cycle of the European great crested newt produces four very different-looking stages—embryo, larva or tadpole, eft, and adult. The journey from tiny white egg to brightly colored 7-in. (17-cm)-long adult takes two to three years. They live underwater for the first few weeks and then metamorphose into land-living juvenile efts. The mature adult newt returns to the water to breed.

As it metamorphoses into an adult, the newt absorbs the gills and becomes bright orange with distinctive black markings.

"Never try to catch two frogs with one hand."

Chinese proverb

The adult newt powers through the water with a wave of its tail.

3. Eft to adult

After about four months, the larvae change, or metamorphose, into an air-breathing form called an eft. They grow legs, their gills change into lungs, and they move onto land, developing fully into adults. They return to the water for a few months each year to breed.

⊖ THE MIDWIFE TOAD

The common midwife toad lives in ponds, streams, and rivers throughout Europe. The male is smaller than the female and plays an unusual role when it comes to breeding. He attaches to his body the egg masses that the female lays and carries them until the eggs hatch. He keeps the eggs moist either by staying somewhere damp or by taking dips in water. The females produce up to four clutches of eggs in the breeding season, so the males are kept busy!

Five male midwife toads carrying egg masses on their bodies.

SELF-PROTECTION

Marine toads can be up to 10 in. (25cm) in length and more than 4 lbs. (2kg) in weight.

It is a dangerous world, and animals need to defend themselves. Some attack before they can be attacked. Many are armed with horns, sharp teeth, quills, claws, or great strength. Some give off powerful smells or simply run away quickly, while others adopt frightening poses. Many amphibians are brightly colored or have poisonous skin that tastes nasty to a predator. There are even toads that play dead!

"Swallow a toad in the morning and you will encounter nothing more disgusting the rest of the day."

Nicolas Chamfort (1741–1794)
French writer and wit

Poisonous prey

The world's largest toad lives in the open grasslands and woodlands of Central and South America and Australia. Called the marine toad and cane toad, it is prey to snakes, caimans, birds of prey, and black rats. If squeezed in their jaws, the toad oozes highly toxic fluid. However, many of its predators are immune to this poison.

Fire salamanders are nocturnal, searching for their insect prey on the forest floor at night.

Poisonous defense

The fire salamander has large glands behind its eyes and down its back on either side of the spine. If the animal is threatened, the glands produce a milky defensive chemical called salamandrin. This poison is strong enough to kill small animals.

> The 2-in. (5-cm)-long golden poison-arrow frog has enough venom to kill ten grown men.

bufotoxins from
glands on shoulders
contain 14 chemicals

http://animals.nationalgeographic.com/animals/amphibians/golden-poison-dart-frog.html

⊖ PLAYING DEAD

When threatened, the Surinam toad
(above) and the leopard frog may play
dead by keeping still. The Surinam
toad is particularly convincing
because it is almost completely flat in
shape and looks like a leaf. It also uses
this ability to hunt, lying still on the
bottom of streams to ambush prey.

Poisonous frogs

The poison-arrow frogs of Central and
South America are protected effectively
against predators such as snakes and
spiders. The frogs are brilliantly colored,
and these "warning colors" alert
predators to the dangers of trying
to pick them up and eat them.
The frogs also secrete deadly
toxins from their skin.

strawberry poison-
arrow frogs in
the rainforest

SWIMMING AND BUOYANCY

Fish swim smoothly through water by contracting and relaxing muscles on each side of their body. This causes waves of movement to travel from the head toward the tail, propelling the fish forward. Different shaped tails help fish travel at different rates. Pectoral and pelvic fins help fish move, maneuver, and stop. Some fish even use them to swim backward. To control buoyancy, most fish are equipped with a gas-filled organ called the swim bladder.

"This is the Ocean, silly, we're not the only two in here."

Dory
fictional fish in the movie **Finding Nemo** *(2003)*

*pectoral fins
flap like wings*

Wings underwater

Manta rays have larger pectoral fins than most fish, and they travel by gracefully flapping them like wings. They feed on plankton and fish larvae filtered from the water passing through their gills. Instead of a swim bladder, rays and sharks have an oil-filled liver that prevents them from sinking.

> Male sea horses carry their young in pouches until they are ready to give birth.

The manta ray filters plankton with its gills.

Oxygen is taken from the water through gills.

dorsal fin

caudal fin

pectoral fin

pelvic fin

backbone

swim bladder

intestines

liver

The swim bladder sits below the backbone of a fish.

Staying afloat

The swim bladder of a fish is a sac inside its abdomen. It contains gas—mostly oxygen but also some nitrogen and carbon dioxide. The fish's body controls the amount of oxygen that enters and exits the sac. This allows the fish to remain at a particular depth or move up or down in the water column.

Triangular pectoral fins form a wingspan of up to 23 ft. (7m).

These longsnout sea horses use their tails to wrap around sea grasses or pieces of coral on the reefs where they live.

Swimming upright

Sea horses do not have caudal fins. They use their dorsal fins to push themselves through the water. This results in their swimming upright and slowly while they steer with pectoral fins on either side of their head.

IN THE DEEP

Light does not penetrate beyond a few hundred yards below the surface of Earth's oceans. In these dark and hostile waters live some of the strangest creatures on the planet. Many of them are fierce predators with sharp teeth, flexible jaws, and unusual hunting strategies. Living at great depths, they are seldom seen, and little is known about their life cycles.

> PHOTOPHORE—*a light-producing organ found in some deep-sea fish*

A 4-in. (10cm)-long female bearded anglerfish, or illuminated netdevil, floats motionless. The bioluminescent lure on its head and barbel (beard) hanging from its chin attract prey toward its gaping jaws.

anglerfish can move and light up their lures when needed

elaborate barbel resembles a piece of seaweed, attracting shrimp and other prey

When the tiny 0.2-in. (6mm)-long male bearded anglerfish finds a female, he bites into her skin and fuses with her, becoming part of her body. This means that, when she is ready to spawn, there is a mate immediately available.

circular photophores behind each eye illuminate the water with a red glow

The stoplight loosejaw dragonfish is unusual—it can produce and see red light. In depths of up to 8,200 ft. (2,500m), it also produces green light from a comma-shaped photophore.

Light in the darkness

Deep-sea fish have adapted in many varied ways to the different depths at which they live. Some species have special organs called photophores that give off bioluminescent light—a light produced by a chemical reaction. Other species have "fishing rods" that act as lures, or long feelers that help them seek out prey.

The living fossil

In 1938, an unusual fish was caught in the western Indian Ocean. It was identified as a coelacanth, which was thought to have been extinct for at least 65 million years. Coelacanths can be up to 6.5 ft. (2m) long and live at depths of up to 2,300 ft. (700m).

third "leg" formed from extended tail fin

The tripodfish lives at the bottom of the ocean. To catch prey, it "stands" on the sea floor, facing into the current and waiting for small crustaceans to be swept toward it.

front "legs" formed from extended pelvic fins

underside is covered in glowing photophores

The cookiecutter shark has been found in water up to 11,480 ft. (3,500m) below the surface. This small shark attaches itself to prey, such as a whale, and spins to cut out a cookie-shaped plug of flesh.

Deep-sea shark

This rarely seen frilled shark looks more like an eel than a shark. It has 300 distinctive pronged teeth and an extraordinary curved tail fin. It is up to 6.5 ft. (2m) long and hunts fish, squid, and other sharks at depths of up to 4,900 ft. (1,500m). This species has changed very little since prehistoric times.

〉 The black seadevil anglerfish is the size of a tennis ball.

LONG-DISTANCE TRAVEL

MIGRATION—*the long-distance movement of an animal from one place to another*

A PLAGUE OF LOCUSTS

The migratory locust migrates when its food supply becomes irregular, usually because of the weather. Swarms are sometimes carried by the wind for up to 300 mi. (500km) in a single night, and when they land, they eat all the vegetation over a vast area. They travel in huge swarms—the largest known swarm contained about 40 billion insects.

Some invertebrates travel great distances at particular times of the year. These migrations can range from a few miles to several thousand miles. Changes in weather and temperature play an important role in stimulating many animals to travel. Some migrations are two-way journeys, with the migrants or their offspring returning to particular breeding areas every year. Some journeys are controlled not by the invertebrates but by the tides or winds.

Spiny lobsters set out on their annual migration in the Bahamas.

They follow the light-colored spots on the lobster in front of them.

"Not all those who wander are lost."

J. R. R. Tolkien (1892–1973)
British writer, from his novel
The Fellowship of the Ring *(1954)*

> In 1988, desert locusts were blown 2,800 mi. (4,500km) from Africa to the West Indies by unusually powerful winds.

http://spaceplace.nasa.gov/migration

One by one

Once a year, large numbers of spiny lobsters move in single file across the sea floor on a migration that takes them from shallow to deep water. In the spring, the spawning season, adult females lay thousands of eggs in warm, coastal areas. Their extraordinary journey usually takes place in the fall, when the lobsters travel to deep water for the winter.

They keep contact with one another by using their antennae.

Tiny travelers

Vertical migration happens in oceans and rivers. Some of the smallest creatures, zooplankton, travel up and down in the water, their movements triggered by light levels. At dusk, they reach the surface to graze on phytoplankton overnight.

Clouds of butterflies

Every year, clouds of beautiful monarch butterflies travel 2,000 mi. (3,200km) from southern Canada to the warmth of central Mexico, where they spend the winter. The following spring, they or their offspring return to Canada, laying eggs on the way.

AMBUSH!

Predatory invertebrates lie in wait for prey, often using camouflage to great effect. Some brightly colored crab spiders look exactly like a flower and inject a powerful poison to kill insects larger than themselves. Assassin bugs stab flies, mosquitoes, and caterpillars, paralyzing them. And ichneumon wasps parasitize their prey, laying their eggs in the larvae and pupae of other insects. The larvae eat their hosts from the inside.

⊖ STABBED TO DEATH

Robber flies sit very still somewhere where they can see all around them with their large eyes. When potential food flies past, these large flies, which are up to 2 in. (5cm) in length, spring off their perch and capture their prey in flight. They have a strong, piercing proboscis and spiny legs that help them hold on to struggling prey.

A robber fly sucks at its blue beetle prey.

An orchid mantis on an orchid flower in Malaysia.

mantis lies in wait looking exactly like a petal

unsuspecting fly is seized when it lands

Predatory mantis

One of the most extraordinary animal camouflages is that of the praying mantis—so called because it holds its front legs up as if it is "praying." These insects live in tropical areas, and individual species are often camouflaged to match plants in their habitat.

 > There are about 37,500 different known species of spiders in the world.

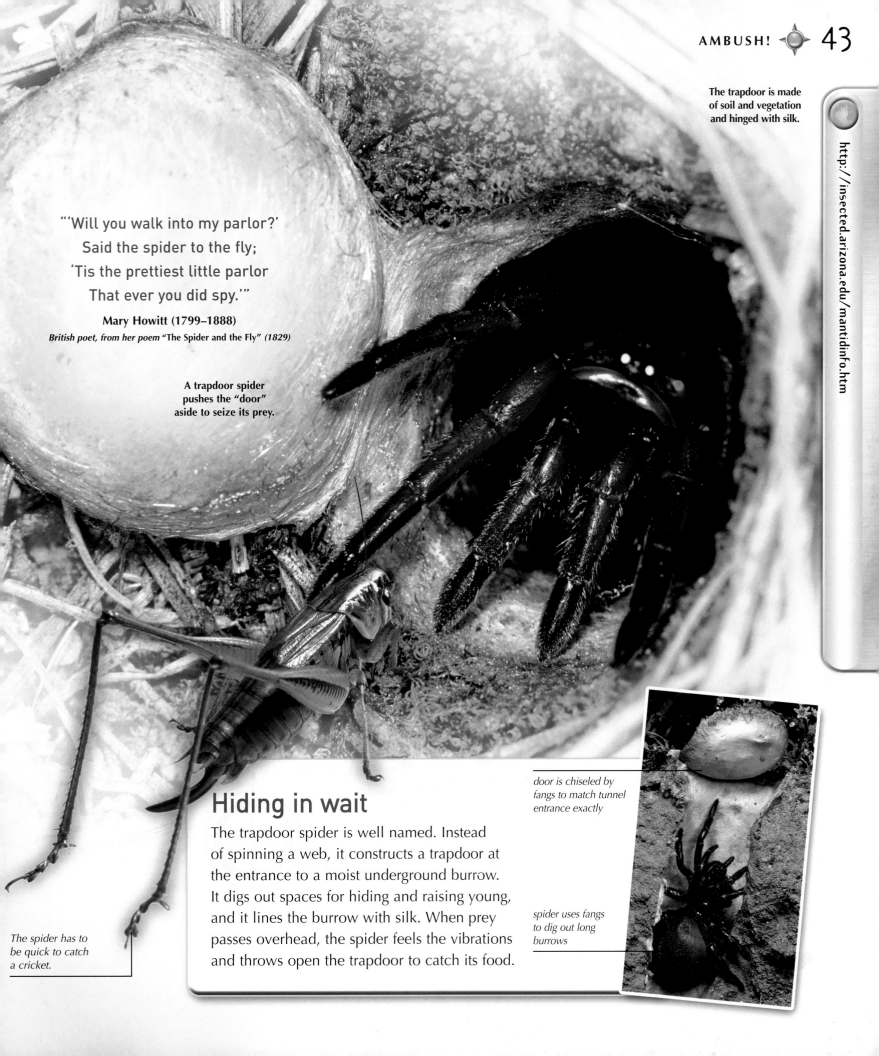

The trapdoor is made of soil and vegetation and hinged with silk.

"'Will you walk into my parlor?'
Said the spider to the fly;
'Tis the prettiest little parlor
That ever you did spy.'"

Mary Howitt (1799–1888)
British poet, from her poem "The Spider and the Fly" (1829)

A trapdoor spider
pushes the "door"
aside to seize its prey.

The spider has to
be quick to catch
a cricket.

Hiding in wait

The trapdoor spider is well named. Instead
of spinning a web, it constructs a trapdoor at
the entrance to a moist underground burrow.
It digs out spaces for hiding and raising young,
and it lines the burrow with silk. When prey
passes overhead, the spider feels the vibrations
and throws open the trapdoor to catch its food.

door is chiseled by
fangs to match tunnel
entrance exactly

spider uses fangs
to dig out long
burrows

GLOSSARY

algae (sing. alga)
Simple nonflowering plants in water without true stems or roots.

antennae (sing. antenna)
A pair of long feelers on an animal's head that are used to obtain information by touch, taste, or smell.

bacterium (pl. bacteria)
A microorganism; some bacteria cause disease.

baleen
The long fibers that hang down like a curtain from a whale's upper jaw and are used to filter food from water.

bioluminescence
The production of light by living things; found in fish and insects as well as simple animals that live in the ocean.

breeding
Producing offspring by mating.

clone
Describes two or more living things that share exactly the same genes.

clutch
A collection of eggs laid at one time by a female animal.

courtship
The behavior that an animal uses to attract a partner in order to mate.

crustacean
An invertebrate with a hard, outer skeleton and jointed limbs; usually found in water.

egg tooth
Hard structure on the beak of hatching birds used to break out of the egg.

embryo
The young of an animal in the earliest stage of development in a womb or egg.

evolved
Gradually changed over time.

extinct
No longer existing or living.

fertilization
The process in which male and female cells join to produce new living things.

forage
To search for food.

gills
Body parts that water-living animals use to collect oxygen from the water.

gland
An organ or group of cells that produces substances needed by the body.

invertebrate
An animal that does not have a backbone.

larva (pl. larvae)
The second stage in the life of an insect, between the egg and the adult.

lek
A place where male animals gather, and sometimes fight, to attract their mates.

litter
A number of young born to an animal at one time.

membrane
A thin layer of animal tissue.

metabolism

The chemical and physical changes that take place in the body, enabling it to grow and function.

metamorphose

To change in body shape; a tadpole metamorphoses into a frog, and a caterpillar metamorphoses into a butterfly.

mimic

An animal that copies another, often in order to avoid being eaten.

molt

To shed an outer covering, such as skin or feathers.

nocturnal

Describes an animal that is active mainly at night and sleeps during the day.

nutrients

Substances taken in by animals that sustain life and help them grow.

paralyze

To make unable to move.

parasitize

To live on another animal, taking nutrients from that animal's body.

phytoplankton

Tiny plants that float in water.

placenta

The organ that supplies oxygen and nutrients to the embryo or fetus during the pregnancy of female mammals.

plankton

Microscopic living animals and plants that drift near the surface of water.

plumage

The covering of feathers on a bird.

prehensile

Describes something that can wrap around an object to hold on to it. Some monkeys, for example, have prehensile tails.

proboscis

A long, flexible snout.

pupa (pl. pupae)

The resting, nonfeeding stage during the life cycle of an insect.

scavenge

To live on dead remains that have been left by predators.

stoop

To swoop down, such as when a hawk dives to catch a rabbit.

talons

The sharp claws of birds of prey. They use them to snatch up their quarry.

ultrasonic

Describes a sound that is higher than a human ear can detect.

vertebrae (sing. vertebra)

Bones that link together to form the backbone, or spine, of an animal.

vertebrate

An animal that has a backbone.

INDEX

INVESTIGATE

Find out how the experts know about animals and explore the natural world by checking out safari parks, books, websites, and museums.

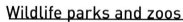

giraffe at a safari park

Wildlife parks and zoos

Visit a wildlife park or zoo and see some of the extraordinary variety of animals that live on Earth. You can also ask experts questions and learn how to take part in conservation projects to protect animals in the wild.

National Geographic Encyclopedia of Animals by Karen McGhee and George McKay (National Geographic Children's Books)

The Bronx Zoo, 2300 Southern Blvd., Bronx, NY 10460

www.sandiegozoo.org/conservation

crimson winged parakeets by author and artist Edward Lear (1812–1888)

Books and magazines

Discover all kinds of facts about animals for yourself by reading information books and magazines about animals.

Navigators: Killer Creatures by Claire Llewellyn (Kingfisher)

Visit your local library to discover a whole range of animal books.

http://kids.nationalgeographic.com/kids

black bears in the American Museum of Natural History

Museums and exhibitions

Visit the many museums and special exhibitions that have interactive displays and give expert information to visitors about all kinds of animals.

Animals at War by Isabel George and Rob Lloyd Jones (Usborne)

National Museum of Natural History, 10th St. and Constitution Ave. NW, Washington, DC 20560

http://fieldmuseum.org/happening/exhibits

emperor penguins marching in front of a camera

Documentaries and movies

There are many animal documentaries on television and movies at the theater that will take you right into the world of your favorite animal.

March of the Penguins (Warner Independent Features and National Geographic Feature Films)

IMAX Dome Theater, Museum of Science and Industry, 4801 E. Fowler Ave., Tampa, FL 33617

www.pbs.org/wnet/nature